Located in Paducah, Kentucky, the American Quilter's Society (AQS) is dedicated to promoting the accomplishments of today's quilters. Through its publications and events, AQS strives to honor today's quiltmakers and their work and to inspire future creativity and innovation in quiltmaking.

EDITOR: HELEN SQUIRE
TECHNICAL EDITOR: BONNIE K. BROWNING
BOOK DESIGN/ILLUSTRATIONS: MICHAEL G. BUCKINGHAM
COVER DESIGN: MICHAEL G. BUCKINGHAM
PHOTOGRAPHY: CHARLES R. LYNCH

Library of Congress Cataloging-in-Publication Data
Buckingham, Michael G.
    Presidential Redwork: A Stitch In Time / Michael G. Buckingham
        p.   cm.
    ISBN 1-57432-744-5
    1. Redwork--Patterns.   2. Traditional History Quilts.   3. American Presidents. 4. Embroidery.
quilts--United States--History.   I. Title.
                                     Applied for.
                                     CIP

Additional copies of this book may be ordered from the American Quilter's Society, PO Box 3290, Paducah, KY 42002-3290 @ $16.95. Add $2.00 for postage and handling.

Copyright ©2000, Michael G. Buckingham

All rights reserved. No part of this book may be reproduced, stored in any retrieval system, or transmitted in any form, or by any means including but not limited to electronic, mechanical, photocopy, recording, or otherwise, without the written consent of the author and publisher. Permission is granted to photocopy patterns for personal use only.

★ ★ ★  Dedication ★ ★ ★

*This book is dedicated to
the memory of my grandfather*

Grover Cleveland Whitaker

★ ★ ★ Acknowledgments ★ ★ ★

I would like to thank the following for their invaluable assistance...

Helen Squire, for her inspiration, creative energy, and for her warm generosity.

Bonnie Browning, for her technical insight and expertise.

Meredith Schroeder and the American Quilter's Society, for the opportunity to do this book.

The Redwork Club of Quilter's Alley and the individual quilters who contributed their time and effort to help make this a better book.

The Presidents of the United States, for their life stories, their example of character (in most), and for their mug-shots, which make great embroidery patterns.

My two sons, Collin and Jacob, for showing me that a book on embroidery patterns can also make a great coloring book, among other things.

My wife, Paulette, for her support, her encouragement, and her much appreciated assistance in gathering and organizing historical information. I love you.

...and most of all, I would like to thank my Heavenly Father, through whom all things are possible.

★★★ Contents ★★★

Introduction 6

Redwork Yesterday & Today 7

Presidential Patterns 17

Historical Designs 61

Quilt Settings & Patterns 71

Bibliography 79

★★★

Introduction ★ ★ ★ ★ ★

Every quilt has a story to tell. The most simple of quilts may tell a tale of hardship or practicality. More exquisite quilts may tell of the person's desire for creative expression. None tell a story better, though, than the redwork embroidery quilts of the late 1800s and early 1900s. This popular fusion of embroidery and quilting was used to record historical events or special occurrences in one's life. Important dates were usually recorded, along with names of people and places. In a sense, they have become historical documents.

The presidential redwork quilts, in my opinion, are the most fascinating of this period. They are fairly easy to date. Judging by the last president embroidered, you can roughly estimate the age of the quilt to within four to eight years. For example, our quilt, from which the following patterns are taken, ends with President Taft. He served from 1909 to 1913, so you can be fairly certain that the quilt was finished within or after that four year period. I am also impressed by the artistic range of portraiture. Earlier presidents seem to be depicted in a more primitive style while later ones appear to be more refined. It is clear, also, that more than one person was involved in embroidering the individual blocks. A project of this magnitude would certainly welcome a number of participants.

In this first election year of the new millennium, it seemed appropriate to continue the presidential redwork tradition with patterns of not only the previously existing blocks but also of every president since, from Woodrow Wilson to Bill Clinton. I also felt that the project would be more fun if you knew more about the lives of the men that you were embroidering. Therefore, a brief biography and timeline have been included with each presidential pattern. Finally learn who is really buried in Grant's Tomb! Be careful, though, that some other family member doesn't run off with your pattern book. Some find it to be enjoyable reading, and my own children think that the patterns make a great coloring book.

Depending on how you decide to arrange your blocks in a quilt setting, you may find it necessary to add some "filler" patterns. A fine assortment of historical and patriotic designs is provided for this purpose. Also included in the book are layout suggestions for your quilt as well as quilting patterns for sashing and borders.

On a personal note, I would like to say that writing this book has been both enjoyable and educational. The most challenging task has been trying to condense each president's amazing or not-so-amazing life into one brief paragraph. I think that you will learn, as I did, a few new facts and develop a deeper appreciation for the men who have held the office of President of the United States.

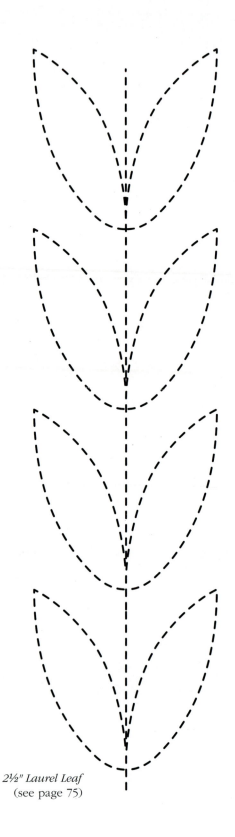

2½" Laurel Leaf
(see page 75)

Redwork
Yesterday & TODAY

★ GALLERY

★ REDWORK TIPS

★ EMBROIDERY ALTERNATIVES

★ SUPPLIES

★ Presidential Redwork Quilt, c.1910 ★

This quilt is similar to those of the period whose patterns were made available at the 1901 Pan American Exposition in Buffalo, New York. Sadly, the expo became famous as the site of President McKinley's assassination.

83" x 90" quilted
From the collection of Helen Squire

★ Points to Consider ★

Although the simple outline (or stem) stitch is preferred, a variety of stitches can be used to attain different line thicknesses without changing thread. Note the chain stitches throughout the hair.

To eliminate "varicose veins," make sure that the back of your block is tidy (see page 13).

This embroiderer lacked an "eye" for detail. For facial features, it is best to stitch with one strand to prevent loss of detail in small areas.

Martin Van Buren
Eighth President of the United States
Quilter Unknown

Faded through the years, this particular information was penned in ink. Other presidential redwork quilts show this part of the pattern either inked or embroidered. Both ways are acceptable – it's a matter of personal taste.

White is nice, but "muslin" is the recommended fabric color. Woven, unbleached muslin has a tendency to shrink, as seen in older redwork quilts, but today's broadcloths (fabric) are dyed a nice antique, off-white shade called muslin.

Diagonal quilting is a simple yet effective way to finish your redwork project. Notice, however, that the quilting stitches do not enter the facial area.

★ Yesterday's ★ Presidential Redwork

HAIR

William Henry Harrison
Ninth President of the United States
Quilter Unknown

One thing hasn't changed throughout the years – politicians still seem to have bad hair cuts (why do you think they used to wear wigs?). The creator of these two blocks overcame that obstacle and did a fine job of hairstyling stitchery.

John Tyler
Tenth President of the United States
Quilter Unknown

10 Presidential Redwork: A Stitch In Time   Michael G. Buckingham

★ Yesterday's ★
Presidential Redwork

BEARDS

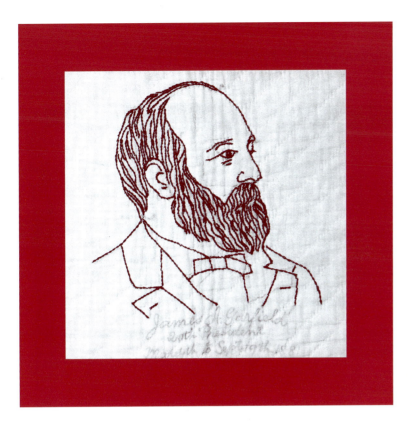

James Garfield
Twentieth President of the United States
Quilter Unknown

There were five bearded presidents, beginning with Abraham LIncoln and ending with Benjamin Harrison. After you have embroidered a couple of these patterns, you'll be glad there were only five. Time and patience, however, will reward your effort with some of your most attractive redwork blocks.

Benjamin Harrison
Twenty-third President of the United States
Quilter Unknown

★ Presidential Redwork Quilt, 2000 ★

61" x 70" unquilted
The Redwork Club of Quilter's Alley
Paducah, Kentucky
Fabrics donated by Peter Pan Fabrics

Presidential Redwork: A Stitch In Time

Michael G. Buckingham

★ Today's ★
Presidential Redwork

Harry S Truman
Thirty-third President of the United States
Ina K. Glick – Metropolis, Illinois

Back detail
Dwight D. Eisenhower
Thirty-fourth President of the United States
Ina K. Glick – Metropolis, Illinois

John F. Kennedy
Thirty-fifth President of the United States
Lorraine Ashby – Metropolis, Illinois

★ Today's ★ Presidential Redwork

Richard M. Nixon
Thirty-seventh President of the United States
Pat Lewis – Paducah, Kentucky

Ronald Reagan
Fortieth President of the United States
Joyce Champion – Paducah, Kentucky

William Jefferson Clinton
Forty-second President of the United States
Victoria Faoro – Paducah, Kentucky

★ Redwork Tips ★

★ Cut background fabric larger than your finished block size. Use an embroidery hoop that is smaller than your fabric square.

★ Re-size patterns as desired to fit within your finished block size. The patterns in this book have been drawn to fit within a 9" block.

★ Carefully position your pattern before tracing. Using a fine-point permanent red marking pen helps hide tracing lines after embroidery is finished (see below).

★ You don't have to embroider every line on a pattern, but remember – if you do trace it onto your fabric, you have to stitch it!

★ For the most authentic color, use DMC #304 embroidery floss. Use 2 or 3 strands to embroider – use one less for facial details.

★ To prevent threads from shadowing as shown on page 9, be sure to knot and trim threads, or bury or travel them in previous stitches (see *Eisenhower back* on page 13).

★ After embroidering, press the block face down into a fluffy towel (without steam), then square-off and trim to finished size.

*The recommended stitch for redwork is the **outline** or **stem stitch**. It can be done with one, two, or three strands of floss to achieve different line widths for various degrees of detail.*

TRANSFERRING THE PATTERN TO FABRIC

With today's electronic equipment it is easier to transfer the pattern to the fabric square. This book has been saddle-stitched so it can be easily opened and placed flat on a photocopier or scanner.

Photocopier Method:

It is legal to photocopy patterns from this book for personal use. Place pattern page face down on the copier, set enlargement or reduction percentage as desired, copy and trace (see page 16 for tracing details).

Scanner Method:

This system transfers the pattern without having to trace. It requires a personal computer, a flat-bed color scanner, appropriate software, and a color inkjet printer. After placing the pattern in the scanner, scan only the pattern area. Make size adjustments to the pattern then flip horizontally with the scanning software. You should now have a mirror image of the pattern. Save the scan, then print the image to paper on the color inkjet printer. You now have an iron-on pattern. For best results, experiment with the actual iron-on procedure. This method not only eliminates tedious tracing, but gives a more accurate and detailed pattern to stitch.

Some printers or color copiers allow you to print directly onto a specially prepared fabric sheet. If such a device is used, do *not* flip the scanned image before printing.

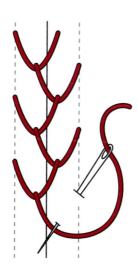

*The **feather stitch** is recommended for embellishing seams between redwork blocks when sashing is not used.*

Other stitches may be used to change line width without changing strand count. See hair detail on page 9.

★ Embroidery ★ Alternatives

"Liquid embroidery" is perfect for school and craft projects using the patterns in this book. It's fast, fun, inexpensive, and provides instant images of Americana without sewing!

★ Enlarge pattern to preferred size.

★ Tape or pin copy of pattern under background fabric.

★ Position over light source (light box, sliding glass door, glass coffee table with lamp underneath, etc.).

★ Copy/trace pattern onto fabric. Use Pigma™ markers in red or black, or a regular lead pencil. Mark lightly.

★ You can immediately outline details with opaque paint markers or three-dimensional paint (available at local art and craft stores) over a light source without tracing first.

★ To apply 3-D paint, work from side to side to prevent smudging. Allow 24 hours to dry.

★ Opaque paint markers may bleed through fabric; take precautions to protect pattern and working surface.

★ Trim block to desired size.

25 Cent Eagle in 3-D paint
17" x 17"
by Vanessa Kaiser

SUPPLIES

- Patterns (actual size or enlarged)
- Light box or other light source
- Marking tools
  - mechanical or #3 lead pencil
  - permanent marker (red or black) Pigma™ Micron 005
- Fabric squares
- Embroidery thread
  - DMC #304 floss
    or substitute
  - Three-dimensional paint
  - Opaque paint markers
- Embroidery hoop
- Embroidery needles (3/9 assorted)
- Small, sharp scissors

Presidential Redwork: A Stitch In Time — Michael G. Buckingham

Presidential
PATTERNS

★ 1789 – 2001

Wooden dentures did not keep the "Father of Our Country" from taking a bite out of British tyranny in America's fight for independence. This great American hero selflessly served his country in many capacities: as soldier, statesman, constitutional leader, and ultimately as the first President of the newly formed United States. Washington was so popular that no other candidate was seriously considered. He is the only American president to have been elected by a unanimous electoral vote. Although he longed for his farm estate on the Potomac, Washington served out his presidency from the temporary U.S. capitals of New York City and Philadelphia. Retiring to his beloved Mount Vernon, he died two short years later.

Notable Inscription: (from the Washington Monument)
Washington, the brave, the wise, the good...father of nations, the friend of mankind...

George Washington
1789 – 1797

Birthplace: Westmoreland Co., Virginia
Born: 1732 **Died**: 1799
Party: Federalist
Terms: Two
Vice-President: John Adams

Cotton Gin 1793

1789 — 2001

George Washington
1st President 1789-1797

Presidential Redwork: A Stitch In Time — Michael G. Buckingham

John Adams
1797 – 1801

Birthplace:
Quincy, Massachusetts

Born: 1735 **Died:** 1826
Party: Federalist
Terms: One
Vice-President:
Thomas Jefferson

A driving force in America's independence movement, John Adams is one of only two presidents whose signature is on the Declaration of Independence. Despite being "obnoxious and unpopular," his energy and great conviction helped to push the Declaration through a divided Continental Congress. Adams served as a foreign diplomat during the Revolutionary War and later as vice-president under George Washington. The first president to lead from the new capital of Washington, D.C., he was also the first to live in the White House and the only president, to date, to father another president.

Notable Quote:
All that I have, all that I am, all that I hope for in this life, I stake on our cause. For me the die is cast. Sink or swim, live or die, to survive or perish with my country is my unalterable resolution!

First Electric Battery 1800

1789   2001

John Adams
2nd President 1797-1801

Farmer, lawyer, scholar, musician, inventor, architect, and statesman, Thomas Jefferson will long be remembered as the author (and a signer) of the Declaration of Independence. He served as governor of Virginia, minister to France, secretary of state to George Washington, and vice-president to John Adams before becoming the third president of the United States. Acquisition of the Louisiana Purchase, more than doubling the size of the country, and the Lewis and Clark Expedition were Jefferson's major presidential achievements. After his presidency he founded the University of Virginia. It seems fitting that Thomas Jefferson died on Independence Day, July 4, 1826, the same day as fellow patriot John Adams.

Notable Quote:
We hold these truths to be self-evident: that all men are created equal...

Thomas Jefferson
1801 – 1809

Birthplace: Albemarle Co., Virginia
Born: 1743 **Died:** 1826
Party: Republican
Terms: Two
Vice-President: Aaron Burr, George Clinton

Fulton's First Steamboat Voyage 1807

1789 2001

Thomas Jefferson
3rd President 1801-1809

James Madison
1809 – 1817

Birthplace:
King George Co., Virginia
Born: 1751 **Died:** 1836
Party: Republican
Terms: Two
Vice-President:
George Clinton, Elbridge Gerry

Although commonly recognized as the husband of Dolly Madison, James Madison is more appropriately honored as the Father of the Constitution. He was instrumental in shaping and ratifying the American Constitution, and later fought to add the Bill of Rights. Madison was Secretary of State under Jefferson, and holds the distinction of being the smallest American president, at 5' 4," never weighing more than 100 pounds. Dolly proved to be a very popular hostess at the White House, which unfortunately was burned by the British during the War of 1812. Madison and his wife had to escape into the nearby woods. In later life, Madison succeeded his good friend Jefferson as rector of the University of Virginia.

Notable Quote:
Oh, I always talk most easily when I lie...said in jest while lying sick in bed

Star-Spangled Banner 1814

1789   2001

James Madison
4th President 1809-1817

22 Presidential Redwork: A Stitch In Time   Michael G. Buckingham

Considered a failure as a foreign minister by two previous administrations, James Monroe as president is best known for the Monroe Doctrine, which since has been the cornerstone of American foreign policy. However, he considered his negotiation of the purchase of the Louisiana Territory under Jefferson as his greatest public service. The last of the founding fathers to serve as president, Monroe fought valiantly in the Revolutionary War under Washington, and was a member of the Continental Congress. He was governor of Virginia, and later Secretary of State and Secretary of War under Madison. A popular president, Monroe gave up only one electoral vote in his bid for re-election. He died on July 4, 1831.

Notable Quote: (by Thomas Jefferson about James Monroe)
...a man whose soul might be turned wrong side outwards without discovering a blemish to the world.

James Monroe
1817 – 1825

Birthplace: Westmoreland Co., Virginia
Born: 1758 **Died**: 1831
Party: Republican
Terms: Two
Vice-President: Daniel D. Tompkins

First Railroad Locomotive 1825

1789　　　　　　　　　　　　　　　　　　　　　　　　　　2001

James Monroe
5th President 1817-1825

Presidential Redwork: A Stitch In Time　　　　　　　Michael G. Buckingham　　23

6 John Quincy Adams
1825 – 1829

Birthplace: Quincy, Massachusetts
Born: 1767 **Died**: 1848
Party: Republican
Terms: One
Vice-President: John C. Calhoun

John Quincy Adams's education in public service started from childhood. Young Quincy would accompany his father on diplomatic missions, and by age 14 was private secretary to the American envoy to Russia. He studied at home and abroad, and like his father had a distinguished career as a foreign diplomat. The younger Adams even served in his father's administration as minister to Prussia. And like his father, he was considered "obnoxious and unpopular" because he did not answer to private interest groups. As president, he established the Smithsonian Institution. His greatest pleasure came after his presidency when the voters in his district elected him to Congress where he served until his death.

Notable Quote: (John Quincy Adams' last words)
Thank the officers of the house. This is the last of earth. I am content.

Invention of Photography 1827

1789   2001

John Quincy Adams
6th President 1825-1829

The first president not of the American "aristocracy," Andrew Jackson was a champion of the common man. The son of poor Irish immigrants, he was born in a log cabin and raised under the greatest of hardships. The colorful Jackson let his fiery temper initiate a number of pistol duels, which seemed to fuel his popularity. He became the first representative to Congress from Tennessee, was a national hero in the War of 1812, and became the first governor of Florida. As president, "Old Hickory" also became the first Democrat in the White House, which was nearly ransacked by his celebrating supporters. Controversial, to say the least, Jackson was responsible for temporarily keeping South Carolina from seceding from the Union.

Notable Quote:
Our Federal Union – it shall and must be preserved!

Andrew Jackson
1829 – 1837

Birthplace: Waxhaw, South Carolina
Born: 1767 **Died**: 1845
Party: Democrat
Terms: Two
Vice-President: John C. Calhoun, Martin Van Buren

McCormick's Reaper 1834

1789 — 2001

Andrew Jackson
7th President 1829-1837

Presidential Redwork: A Stitch In Time — Michael G. Buckingham

Martin Van Buren
1837 – 1841

Birthplace: Kinderhook, New York
Born: 1782 **Died:** 1862
Party: Democrat
Terms: One
Vice-President: Richard M. Johnson

Born after American independence, Martin Van Buren grew up speaking Dutch as his first language. An ambitious politician, he served New York as a state senator, Attorney General, and after an eight-year stint in the U.S. Senate, as governor. An important force in the election of Andrew Jackson, Van Buren served only two months as governor before becoming Jackson's Secretary of State. He was vice-president during Jackson's second term and was one of only four incumbent vice-presidents to be elected to the presidency. His non-handling of an economic depression made him highly unpopular. Soundly defeated in the next election, Van Buren ran again and lost in 1848 on a third-party ticket.

Notable Quote:
...the less Government interferes with private pursuits, the better for general prosperity.

Queen Victoria Crowned 1837

1789　　　　　　　　　　　　　　　　　　　　　　　　　　　　　　　　2001

Martin Van Buren
8th President 1837-1841

26　Presidential Redwork: A Stitch In Time　　　　　　　　Michael G. Buckingham

"Tippecanoe and Tyler, Too!" was the famous campaign cry of William Henry Harrison, who holds the unfortunate distinction of being the first president to die in office. He expired from pneumonia only a month after his inauguration. Ballyhooed as a man of log cabins and cider, Harrison was the son of Benjamin Harrison, Virginia aristocrat, signer of the Declaration of Independence, and governor of Virginia. The younger Harrison served in the administrations of Adams, Jefferson, and Madison, dealing with Indian affairs in the Northwest Territory. As a soldier, General Harrison squashed a major Indian uprising at Tippecanoe and became a national hero when he defeated the British and Indian forces in Canada in the War of 1812.

Notable Quote:
To be eminently great it is necessary to be eminently good.

William Henry Harrison

Mar. 4–April 4, 1841

Birthplace: Charles City Co., Virginia
Born: 1773 **Died**: 1841
Party: Whig
Terms: One month
Vice-President: John Tyler

Dr. Livingstone Arrives in Africa 1841

1789   2001

William Henry Harrison
9th President March - April 1841

Presidential Redwork: A Stitch In Time   Michael G. Buckingham

John Tyler
1841 – 1845

Birthplace:
Charles City Co., Virginia
Born: 1790 **Died**: 1862
Party: Whig
Terms: One
Vice-President: None

John Tyler was the first to succeed from the vice-presidency to the presidency through the death of his predecessor. Much to the displeasure of Harrison's cabinet, Tyler established a precedent by taking the full powers of the presidential office. Tyler fathered more children than any other president, eight by his first wife, who died the second year of his presidency, and seven by his second. Unpopular and considered a weak president, this Virginia gentleman had previously been a U.S. Congressman, Virginia governor, then U.S. Senator. After his presidency, Tyler headed a peace mission from the South which failed. Advocating secession, he was elected to the Confederate Congress but soon died a "rebel."

Notable Quote:
I am president and I shall be held responsible for my administration.

Telegraph Invented 1844

1789   2001

John Tyler
10th President 1841-1845

Presidential Redwork: A Stitch In Time   Michael G. Buckingham

Elected to office during a stretch of "weak" presidents, James Polk is considered to be one of the nation's most successful. He entered his administration with four major objectives and had attained them all by the end of one term. One of these was the acquisition of California, which came about as a result of the controversial Mexican War. Polk was responsible for adding more territory to the United States than any president since Thomas Jefferson. Former governor of Tennessee and seven term U.S. Congressman, Polk is the only president to have previously been the Speaker of the House. Overworked and caught in a cholera epidemic, he died three months after he left office.

Notable Quote:
I prefer to supervise the whole operations of the Government myself...

James K. Polk
1845 – 1849

Birthplace: Mecklenburg Co., NC
Born: 1795 **Died**: 1849
Party: Democrat
Terms: One
Vice-President: George M. Dallas

Texas Annexed 1845

1789 — 2001

James K. Polk
11th President 1845-1849

Presidential Redwork: A Stitch In Time — Michael G. Buckingham

Zachary Taylor
1849 – 1850

Birthplace:
Orange Co., Virginia

Born: 1784 **Died:** 1850

Party: Whig

Terms: 1½ years

Vice-President:
Millard Fillmore

A career soldier, Zachary Taylor was the first of only three men to become president without holding prior public office. The son of a Revolutionary War hero, he embarked on a military career that spanned more than four decades. During those years, Taylor never lost a battle. "Old Rough and Ready" distinguished himself in the War of 1812, and the Mexican War made him a national hero. Despite his military success, he detested war. As president, although a Southerner and a slaveholder, Taylor remained committed to the preservation of the Union. Unfortunately, like fellow Whig Harrison, he died while in office. Future "presidents" that served under Taylor's military command — Lincoln, Grant, and son-in-law Jefferson Davis.

Notable Quote:
My life has been devoted to arms, yet I look upon war at all times...as a national calamity...

California Gold Rush 1849

1789   2001

Zachary Taylor
12th President 1849-1850

30 Presidential Redwork: A Stitch In Time   Michael G. Buckingham

Millard Fillmore was the second vice-president to succeed to the presidency through the death of the current office holder, and the last Whig to hold the office. Born in a log cabin in frontier New York, Fillmore went from poor farmer's son hired into servitude to successful lawyer, holder of various New York public offices, U.S. Congressman, vice-president, and eventually president of the United States. He supported the controversial Compromise of 1850 which kept the nation out of civil war for another 10 years. A highlight of his presidency, Fillmore sent Commodore Perry on a productive mission to open trade with Japan. Wife Abigail's contribution to the White House was surprisingly the first bathtub and the first library.

Notable Quote: (upon declining an honorary degree from Oxford University)
I had not the advantage of a classical education and no man should...accept a degree he cannot read.

Millard Fillmore 13
1850 – 1853

Birthplace: Cayuga Co., New York
Born: 1800 **Died**: 1874
Party: Whig
Terms: 2½ years
Vice-President: None

Uncle Tom's Cabin 1852

1789 — 2001

Millard Fillmore
13th President 1850-1853

Presidential Redwork: A Stitch In Time — Michael G. Buckingham

Franklin Pierce
1853 – 1857

Birthplace: Hillsboro, New Hampshire
Born: 1804 **Died:** 1869
Party: Democrat
Terms: One
Vice-President: William R. King

College classmate of Nathaniel Hawthorne and Henry Wadsworth Longfellow, Franklin Pierce was only twenty-nine when elected to the U.S. Congress. Four years later he was the youngest ever to be elected to the U.S. Senate. Personal tragedy and his wife's disdain for Washington temporarily ended his political career. The son of a Revolutionary War general, Pierce enlisted in the army during the onset of the Mexican War and was appointed brigadier general. He served with distinction, which helped lead to his nomination as a reluctant presidential candidate. As president he was considered to be a "pro-slavery yankee," feeling that slavery was a necessary evil to keep the Union intact.

Notable Quote:
...I have been borne to a position so suitable to others rather than desirable to myself.

Pasteurization of Milk 1856

1789 — 2001

Franklin Pierce
14th President 1853-1857

Presidential Redwork: A Stitch In Time — Michael G. Buckingham

Life-long bachelor James Buchanan had a distinguished political career in all but the presidency. Buchanan had served in the Pennsylvania legislature, U.S. Congress, U.S. Senate, was Jackson's Minister to Russia, Polk's Secretary of State, and Pierce's Minister to England. He had long aspired to be president but finally entered the office in a time of great national crisis. He was considered a success in social and foreign affairs, thanks in part to his niece Harriet Lane, who served as his official hostess. In domestic affairs, however, "Old Buck" was unable to cope with the dilemma at hand. His wait-and-see attitude and indecisiveness over the slavery issue only helped to speed the inevitable breakup of the Union.

Notable Quote: (to Abraham Lincoln upon leaving the White House)

If you are as happy, my dear sir, on entering this house as I am on leaving it…you are the happiest man in the country.

James Buchanan
1857 – 1861

15

Birthplace: Franklin Co., Pennsylvania
Born: 1791 **Died**: 1868
Party: Democrat
Terms: One
Vice-President: John C. Breckenridge

First Successful Oil Well 1859

1789　　2001

James Buchanan
15th President 1857-1861

Abraham Lincoln
1861 – 1865

Born in a log cabin in the wild country of Kentucky, Abraham Lincoln rose from the hardship of frontier life to the highest office of the land. A voracious reader, Lincoln was virtually self-educated and more than handy with an ax. The "rail splitter" was a masterful storyteller, and could "outrun, whip, or throw down any man" around. Lincoln the backwoodsman eventually grew into Lincoln the lawyer. "Honest Abe" served in the Illinois state legislature and the U.S. Congress before his rise to the presidency. Lincoln preserved the Union, nobly leading the broken nation through four years of civil war and finally ending its legacy of slavery. The first president to be assassinated, Abraham Lincoln now "belongs to the ages."

Birthplace: Hardin Co. (now Larue Co.), Kentucky
Born: 1809 **Died:** 1865
Party: Republican (1st term) National Unionist (2nd term)
Terms: One, plus 1½ mos.
Vice-President: Hannibal Hamlin, Andrew Johnson

Notable Quote: (An early comment on slavery)
By God, boys, let's get away from this. If ever I get a chance to hit that thing, I'll hit it hard!

American Civil War
1861–1865

1789 — 2001

Abraham Lincoln
16th President 1861-1865

Presidential Redwork: A Stitch In Time — Michael G. Buckingham

Andrew Johnson has probably been the most unjustly maligned president to hold the office. Inheriting the colossal task of cleaning up the aftermath of the Civil War, Johnson adopted Lincoln's policy of conciliation and restoration. This did not set well with Congress, who wanted to treat the South like a conquered foe. In a purely political move, Congress began the first impeachment proceedings against a U.S. president, falling one vote short of removing Johnson from office. During Lincoln's first term, the "Tennessee Tailor" was the only Southern senator who did not resign and side with his seceding state. However, Johnson reconciled with the people of Tennessee and became the only ex-president to become U.S. Senator.

Notable Quote:
May peace and unison be restored to the land! May God bless this people and save the Constitution!

Andrew Johnson 1865 – 1869

Birthplace: Raleigh, North Carolina
Born: 1808 **Died**: 1875
Party: National Unionist
Terms: 3 years, 10½ mos.
Vice-President: None

U.S. Purchases Alaska 1867

1789 — 2001

Andrew Johnson
17th President 1865-1869

Ulysses S. Grant
1869 – 1877

Birthplace: Point Pleasant, Ohio
Born: 1822 **Died:** 1885
Party: Republican
Terms: Two
Vice-President: Schuyler Colfax, Henry Wilson

Born Hiram Ulysses Grant, the eighteenth president of the United States was mistakenly registered upon entering West Point as Ulysses Simpson Grant. Preferring it to his birth name, he used it the rest of his life. Grant was a mediocre student but an excellent horseman. This served the young officer well in the Mexican War, where he learned firsthand the strategies that helped him lead the Union forces to victory in the Civil War. Nicknamed "Unconditional Surrender," Grant became the first four-star general in U.S. history and a global hero. As president, his administration was marred by corruption from appointees he trusted. Grant's Tomb in New York City is the final resting place of both Grant and his dear wife Julia.

Notable Quote:
I am in for the war and shall stay until this wicked rebellion is crushed...

Custer's Defeat at Little Bighorn 1876

1789 — 2001

Ulysses S. Grant
18th President 1869-1877

Presidential Redwork: A Stitch In Time — Michael G. Buckingham

The outcome of the election of 1876 was not known until two days before Inauguration Day, when Rutherford B. Hayes, winning by one questionable electoral vote, was sworn in as president. Rumors of fraud made him unpopular with the people at first, and sweeping reforms made him unpopular with his party, but these same reforms are what finally endeared him to the nation. Hayes removed the remaining Federal troops from the South, thus ending Reconstruction and speeding the healing of the Union. Before the presidency, he had served as a major general in the Civil War, a U.S. Congressman, and three-time governor of Ohio. The first telephone in the White House was installed during his single term.

Notable Quote:
He serves his party best who serves his country best.

Rutherford B. Hayes
1877 – 1881

Birthplace: Delaware, Ohio
Born: 1822 **Died**: 1893
Party: Republican
Terms: One
Vice-President: William A. Wheeler

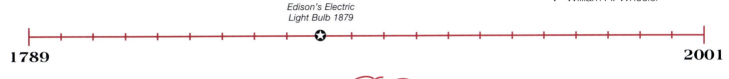
Edison's Electric Light Bulb 1879
1789 — 2001

Rutherford B. Hayes
19th President 1877-1881

Presidential Redwork: A Stitch In Time — Michael G. Buckingham

James A. Garfield
Mar. 4–Sept. 19, 1881

Birthplace: Cuyahoga Co., Ohio
Born: 1831 **Died:** 1881
Party: Republican
Terms: 6 months
Vice-President: Chester A. Arthur

There is not much to be said about the short administration of James Garfield except that he spent most of his time besieged by hungry office-seekers. It was one of these disgruntled applicants who, on July 2, 1881, fired two shots into the President while he was waiting in a Washington train depot. Garfield lingered for two months before finally dying at the age of 49. Garfield was the last president to be born in a log cabin, growing up on a frontier farm in Ohio. By age 26 he was a college president. He was the youngest brigadier general of the Civil War and served as a U.S. representative for 17 years. Sometimes he would entertain fellow congressmen by simultaneously writing Greek with his left hand and Latin with his right.

Notable Quote: (upon word of Lincoln's assassination)
...Fellow citizens, God reigns and the Government at Washington still lives!

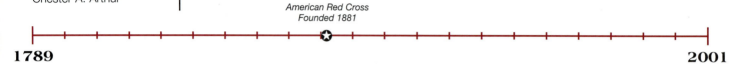

American Red Cross Founded 1881

1789 — 2001

James A. Garfield
20th President March - Sept. 1881

The son of an Irish minister, Chester A. Arthur was born and raised in the Green Mountain country of Vermont. As a school teacher, he once taught at the same school with running-mate James Garfield. Arthur made a fortune in New York as a lawyer, then during the Civil War handled the task of New York's Quartermaster General effectively and without scandal. After the war, Arthur developed a close association with Republican boss Roscoe Conkling, who was responsible for his vice-presidential nomination. When Arthur succeeded Garfield, Conkling found that Arthur had a mind of his own, carrying out civil service reform and running an honest and efficient administration. Arthur also began modernization of the American Navy.

Notable Quote:
If I had misappropriated five cents, and...saw two men talking on the street together, I would imagine they were talking of my dishonesty.

Chester A. Arthur
1881 – 1885

21

Birthplace: Fairfield, Vermont
Born: 1830 **Died**: 1886
Party: Republican
Terms: 3½ years
Vice-President: None

First Skyscraper
1885

1789   2001

Chester A. Arthur
21st President 1881-1885

Presidential Redwork: A Stitch In Time — Michael G. Buckingham

Grover Cleveland
1885 – 1889

Birthplace:
Caldwell, New Jersey

Born: 1837 **Died:** 1908

Party: Democrat

Terms: Two (non-consecutive)

Vice-President:
Thomas A. Hendricks
(First term only)

Born Stephen Grover Cleveland, the future president was the son of a poor Presbyterian minister. As a child, honesty became an important principle in his life. Cleveland never attended college, but after moving to Buffalo, New York, he studied law and was admitted to the bar. By 1881 he was mayor of Buffalo, 1882, governor of New York, and 1884, candidate for the U.S. presidency. A man of character, Cleveland's campaign was not without scandal. He took a firm stand against corruption and extravagance and exercised his veto regularly. He entered the White House as a bachelor, but left as a married man. Upon leaving, his wife said, "Take good care of the furniture...We are coming back just four years from today."

Notable Quote:
I have only one thing to do and that is to do right...

Statue of Liberty 1886

1789 — 2001

Grover Cleveland
22nd President 1885-1889

Presidential Redwork: A Stitch In Time — Michael G. Buckingham

Benjamin Harrison was the grandson of the ninth president of the United States, William Henry Harrison, and the last of the bearded presidents. Born in Ohio on the family homestead, he married and moved to Indianapolis where he began his legal career. At the onset of the Civil War, Harrison raised a regiment of volunteers, leaving the war as a brigadier general and the White House as the last Civil War general to hold the office. During his administration the Oklahoma territory was opened to public settlement and six new states joined the Union. Harrison was the first president to enjoy the luxury of electric lights in the White House, and had the first billion-dollar budget in American history.

Notable Quote:
I want it understood that I am the grandson of nobody. I believe that every man should stand on his own merits.

Benjamin Harrison 1889 – 1893 — 23

Birthplace: North Bend, Ohio
Born: 1833 **Died**: 1901
Party: Republican
Terms: One
Vice-President: Levi P. Morton

Invention of Motion Pictures 1893

1789 — 2001

Benjamin Harrison
23rd President 1889-1893

Presidential Redwork: A Stitch In Time — Michael G. Buckingham

24 Grover Cleveland
1893 – 1897

Birthplace:
Caldwell, New Jersey

Born: 1837 **Died:** 1908

Party: Democrat

Terms: Two (non-consecutive)

Vice-President:
Adlai E. Stevenson
(Second term only)

Surprise! Mrs. Cleveland's parting statement proved to be prophetic. Few people realize that Grover Cleveland served two non-consecutive terms, and in doing so he has created a small technical problem. We say that Bill Clinton is the forty-second president of the United States, but in actuality there have only been forty-one presidents. So as not to re-write American history and disturb the status quo, we'll count Grover twice and say that there are forty-two. Cleveland's second administration was marred by a serious economic depression. On a lighter note, daughter Esther became the first President's child to be born in the White House, and eldest daughter Ruth has been immortalized with the "Baby Ruth" candy bar.

Notable Quote:

I am not concerning myself with what history will think, but...with the approval of a fellow named Cleveland.

First Modern Olympics 1896

1789 — 2001

Grover Cleveland
24th President 1893-1897

42 Presidential Redwork: A Stitch In Time   Michael G. Buckingham

William McKinley was the last Civil War veteran to hold America's highest office. Enlisting as a private, he gained high praise from commanding officer Rutherford B. Hayes, and had achieved the rank of major by war's end. McKinley served over a decade in Congress as well as two terms as governor of Ohio. During his presidency the United States became a world power, acquiring Guam, Puerto Rico, and the Philippines in the Spanish-American War. McKinley was re-elected for a second term in 1901 but was only able to serve six short months of it. While visiting the opening of the Pan-American Exposition in Buffalo, New York, he was shot point-blank by a deranged anarchist. Eight days later he was dead.

Notable Quote: (in reference to his assassin)
Don't let them hurt him. Go easy with him, boys.

William McKinley
1897 – 1901

Birthplace: Niles, Ohio
Born: 1843 **Died**: 1901
Party: Republican
Terms: One, plus 6 months
Vice-President: Garret A. Hobart, Theodore Roosevelt

Marconi's Radio 1901

1789   2001

William McKinley
25th President 1897-1901

Presidential Redwork: A Stitch In Time   Michael G. Buckingham

26 Theodore Roosevelt
1901 – 1909

Birthplace: New York City, New York
Born: 1858 **Died**: 1919
Party: Republican
Terms: One, plus 3½ years
Vice-President: Charles W. Fairbanks *(Second term only)*

Big-game hunter, conservationist, cowboy: these are just a few of the words that describe Theodore Roosevelt, one of our country's most colorful figures. During the Spanish-American War, Roosevelt resigned as Assistant Secretary of the Navy to raise a company of "Rough Riders" which he led in the infamous charge up San Juan Hill. Becoming a national hero, Teddy was elected governor of New York and then went on to become vice-president under William McKinley. He became president upon McKinley's assassination and was later elected to a full term. His most noted accomplishments as Commander-in-Chief were the completion of the Panama Canal and lending his name to the Teddy Bear.

Notable Quote:
Speak softly and carry a big stick...

Wright Brothers' First Flight 1903

1789   2001

Theodore Roosevelt
26th President 1901-1909

44   Presidential Redwork: A Stitch In Time   Michael G. Buckingham

Undoubtedly the largest Commander-in-Chief, William Howard Taft was over six feet tall and weighed well over three hundred pounds. He was a good-natured man who had a heart as big as his frame. As the first governor of the Philippines, Taft turned down two coveted appointments to the Supreme Court to finish his work with his Filipino "brothers." As Roosevelt's Secretary of War, he was groomed for the presidency. As president, he was the first to play golf and the first to own a car, four to be precise. After the presidency, Taft finally realized his life-long dream – Chief Justice of the Supreme Court, thus becoming the only person in the United States to have held both the highest executive and judicial offices.

Notable Quote:
Next to my wife and children, the Court is the nearest thing to my heart.

William Howard Taft
27
1909 – 1913

Birthplace: Cincinnati, Ohio
Born: 1857 **Died**: 1930
Party: Republican
Terms: One
Vice-President: James S. Sherman

Sinking of the Titanic 1912

1789 — 2001

William Howard Taft
27th President 1909-1913

Presidential Redwork: A Stitch In Time — Michael G. Buckingham

28 Woodrow Wilson
1913 – 1921

Birthplace: Staunton, Virginia
Born: 1856 **Died:** 1924
Party: Democrat
Terms: Two
Vice-President: Thomas R. Marshall

Woodrow Wilson is known as the "schoolmaster" president, having been a professor of history and an Ivy League college president, and was the only president to have earned his Ph.D. Wilson was raised in the South, but became the governor of New Jersey while making a name for himself as head administrator at Princeton. His record of fighting corruption gained national attention and helped land him in the White House. Keeping the nation out of the war in Europe, Wilson was elected to a second term. Less than a year later, America was thrust into the "war to end all wars." After Germany's defeat, Wilson was responsible for the formation of the League of Nations, the ill-fated forerunner of the United Nations.

Notable Quote:
I not only use all the brains I have but all I can borrow.

World War I Begins 1914

1789 — 2001

Woodrow Wilson
28th President 1913-1921

Presidential Redwork: A Stitch In Time   Michael G. Buckingham

In the aftermath of World War I and the disillusionment with Wilson's administration, it is said that any Republican could have won the presidency in the 1920 election, and such was the case with Warren G. Harding. Not the typical politician, he was a newspaper publisher and editor most of his life. Harding made some excellent Cabinet appointments, one of which was future president Herbert Hoover. He also made some bad ones, resulting in corruption which has had no equal since the Grant administration. Prohibition was in full swing and the nation was suffering from an economic depression. The combination of these things took its toll on the president's health – two years into his administration, Harding was dead.

Notable Quote: (to Will Rogers upon his visit to the White House)
This is the first time I ever got to see you without paying for it.

Warren G. Harding 29
1921 – 1923

Birthplace: Blooming Grove, Ohio
Born: 1865 **Died**: 1923
Party: Republican
Terms: 2 years
Vice-President: Calvin Coolidge

King Tut's Tomb Discovered 1922

1789 — 2001

Warren G. Harding
29th President 1921-1923

Presidential Redwork: A Stitch In Time — Michael G. Buckingham — 47

Calvin Coolidge
1923 – 1929

Birthplace: Plymouth, Vermont
Born: 1872 **Died:** 1933
Party: Republican
Terms: One, plus 1½ years
Vice-President: Charles G. Dawes *(Second term only)*

At his father's Vermont farm, Calvin Coolidge was awakened in the dead of night to find that he had become the sixth vice-president in American history to be propelled into the presidency by the death of the chief executive. By the light of a kerosene lantern, his father, a notary, administered the oath of office. As president, Coolidge cleaned up the corruption that was prevalent during Harding's administration. He was as frugal with the nation's money as he was with his own, cutting the national debt by two billion dollars. The country was experiencing a post-war boom and Coolidge was elected for a second term. Choosing not to run for a third, he left the presidency more popular than when he had begun.

Notable Quote:
When a great many people are unable to find work, unemployment results.

Lindbergh's Transatlantic Flight 1927

1789 — 2001

Calvin Coolidge
30th President 1923-1929

Presidential Redwork: A Stitch In Time — Michael G. Buckingham

The first president born west of the Mississippi River, Herbert Hoover was the son of a Quaker blacksmith. By the age of 40, he was a multimillionaire, having established gold mining operations around the globe. World War I found Hoover in England, where he became administrator of numerous relief operations. A great humanitarian, he would later play a similar role in relief operations in Europe after World War II. Hoover entered the White House with the largest electoral majority since Washington, yet the greatest economic depression in history ruined his bid for re-election. Hoover was able to do more in retirement than any other president and lived to be 90, longer than any other president since John Adams.

Notable Quote:
(Fishing) is a discipline in the quality of men – for all men are equal before fish.

Herbert Hoover 31
1929 – 1933

Birthplace: West Branch, Iowa
Born: 1874 **Died**: 1964
Party: Republican
Terms: One
Vice-President: Charles Curtis

The Great Depression 1929

1789 — 2001

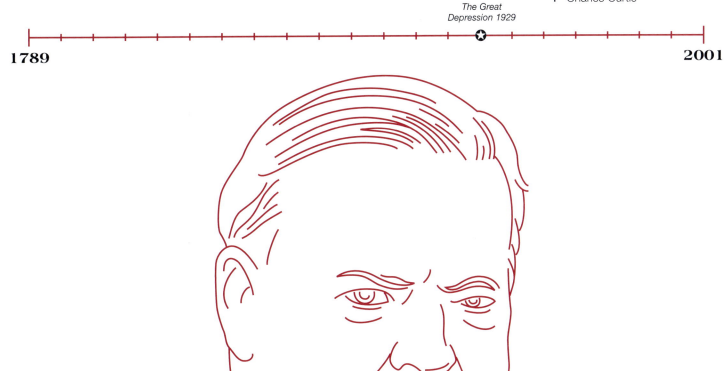

Herbert Hoover
31st President 1929-1933

Presidential Redwork: A Stitch In Time — Michael G. Buckingham

Franklin D. Roosevelt
1933 – 1945

Birthplace: Hyde Park, New York
Born: 1882 **Died:** 1945
Party: Democrat
Terms: Three, plus 1 month
Vice-President: John N. Garner, Henry A. Wallace, Harry S. Truman

Franklin Delano Roosevelt had the longest term of office of any U.S. president. In the twelve years of his administration, the distant cousin of Theodore Roosevelt initiated a broad range of social reforms and established numerous federal agencies to promote the nation's economic recovery. Prohibition was repealed and Social Security was enacted. Roosevelt was the first president to appear on TV and to appoint a female Cabinet member. After the Japanese attack on Pearl Harbor in 1941, America could no longer stay out of the war. FDR valiantly led the nation in the war effort. He also played a principal role in the establishment of the United Nations. Before war's end, Roosevelt died one month into his fourth term.

Notable Quote:
...the only thing we have to fear is fear itself.

World War II
1939–1945

1789   2001

Franklin D. Roosevelt
32nd President 1933-1945

50   Presidential Redwork: A Stitch In Time   Michael G. Buckingham

Harry S Truman was the first and only U.S. president to order the use of an atomic weapon in wartime. The use of the atomic bomb put an immediate end to the war in the Pacific and thus World War II. The first president of the Atomic Age was born the son of a Missouri horse trader and was a farmer himself. Harry (the "S" stands for nothing) Truman served in World War I as an artilleryman, leaving as a Reserve major. His political career started in county government where he established his reputation for honesty. Truman was a popular U.S. Senator during World War II. As vice-president, he succeeded to office upon the death of FDR, and won a second term in the famous "Dewey Defeats Truman" election.

Notable Quote:
The buck stops here!

Harry S Truman 33
1945 – 1953

Birthplace: Lamar, Missouri
Born: 1884 **Died**: 1972
Party: Democrat
Terms: Two
Vice-President: Alben W. Barkley *(second term only)*

Korean War 1950-1953

1789 — 2001

Harry S Truman
33rd President 1945-1953

Presidential Redwork: A Stitch In Time — Michael G. Buckingham

34 | Dwight D. Eisenhower
1953 – 1961

Birthplace:
Denison, Texas

Born: 1890 **Died:** 1969

Party: Republican

Terms: Two

Vice-President:
Richard M. Nixon

When Dwight D. Eisenhower entered the White House, he, like Ulysses S. Grant, had never previously held public office. Also like Grant, he graduated from West Point. A career Army officer, Eisenhower saw no action during World War I, but in the second world war was appointed Supreme Allied Commander in Europe. He returned home a global hero, again not unlike General Grant. He was made General of the Army (five stars) and Supreme Commander of NATO. "Ike" was so popular that both times he ran for the Oval Office, he enjoyed landslide victories. Unlike President Grant, however, Eisenhower was an able administrator. During his administration the space race began, Hawaii and Alaska became states, and the nation prospered.

Notable Quote:
I think that people want peace so much that one of these days governments had better get out of their way and let them have it.

Sputnik Launched 1957

1789 — 2001

Dwight D. Eisenhower
34th President 1953-1961

52   Presidential Redwork: A Stitch In Time   Michael G. Buckingham

The first Roman Catholic U.S. President, John F. Kennedy was also the youngest president elected to office. Kennedy came from a prominent Massachusetts family of Irish descent and was a popular Congressman and Senator from that state. He was a highly decorated veteran of World War II, severely wounded while serving in the South Pacific as a PT boat commander. Kennedy appeared in the first televised presidential debates. As president, he narrowly averted a nuclear conflict during the Cuban missile crisis. Kennedy established the Peace Corp, initiated major civil rights reforms, and promoted the space program. On November 22, 1963, he became the fourth American president to be assassinated.

Notable Quote:
And so, my fellow Americans, ask not what your country can do for you – ask what you can do for your country.

John F. Kennedy 35
1961–Nov. 1963

Birthplace: Brookline, Massachusetts
Born: 1917   **Died**: 1963
Party: Democrat
Terms: 2 years, 10 mos.
Vice-President: Lyndon B. Johnson

First American In Space 1961

1789 — 2001

John F. Kennedy
35th President 1961-1963

Presidential Redwork: A Stitch In Time — Michael G. Buckingham

36 Lyndon B. Johnson
1963 – 1969

Birthplace: Gillespie Co., Texas

Born: 1908 **Died:** 1973

Party: Democrat

Terms: One & 1½ years

Vice-President: Hubert H. Humphrey *(Second term only)*

Before the presidency, Lyndon Baines Johnson had already had an illustrious political career. When war was declared in 1941, he was the first member of Congress to enter active duty and won the Silver Star in the Navy. A disciple of FDR, Johnson had served in the House twelve years, the Senate twelve years, and had been the youngest and most powerful majority leader in the Senate. As vice-president he worked very closely with JFK, and as president was able to push through domestic programs that his predecessor could not. Johnson was the first to appoint an African-American to a Cabinet position and to the Supreme Court. His popularity diminished by the Vietnam War, Johnson did not seek a second full term.

Notable Quote:

I will do my best. That is all I can do. I ask your help – and God's.

Martin Luther King, Jr. Assassinated 1968

1789 — 2001

Lyndon B. Johnson

36th President 1963-1969

Of humble Quaker origins, Richard Milhous Nixon was born on a lemon grove in southern California. He was an accomplished debater and class leader in college and law school. During World War II he served as an operations officer in the Navy. After the war Nixon began his political career, winning a seat in Congress and eventually the Senate. He served two terms as vice-president in the Eisenhower administration. As president, he initiated the end of U.S. involvement in the Vietnam War, and did much for foreign affairs. Scandal disrupted Nixon's second term. Vice-President Spiro Agnew resigned due to income tax evasion. Nixon's involvement in the Watergate scandal led him to become the only president in U.S. history to resign.

Notable Quote:
...if some of my judgments were wrong, and some were wrong, they were made in what I believed at the time to be the best interest of the Nation.

Richard M. Nixon — 37

1969 – Aug. 1974

Birthplace: Yorba Linda, California
Born: 1913 **Died**: 1994
Party: Republican
Terms: One, plus 1½ years
Vice-President: Spiro T. Agnew, Gerald R. Ford

First Manned Moon Landing 1969

1789 — 2001

Richard M. Nixon
37th President 1969-1974

Presidential Redwork: A Stitch In Time — Michael G. Buckingham

Gerald R. Ford

Aug. 1974 – 1977

Birthplace: Omaha, Nebraska
Born: 1913
Party: Republican
Terms: 2½ years
Vice-President: Nelson A. Rockefeller

When President Ford first took office, it was obvious that his administration would have to be a time of healing. One of his first actions was to issue a full pardon to former President Nixon. When Nelson Rockefeller took his oath, it was the only time that both the president and vice-president had not been elected by the people. Despite this fact, Ford was a capable president. He had been a respected long-time member and minority leader of the House when appointed as Nixon's VP. During World War II, Ford served in the Navy as a lieutenant commander, and before that was a football all-star at the University of Michigan. Due mainly to high unemployment, Ford was never an elected president, losing to Jimmy Carter in 1976.

Notable Quote: (after Nixon's resignation)
Our long national nightmare is over...Our Constitution works.

First Personal Computer 1975

1789 — 2001

Gerald R. Ford
38th President 1974-1977

56 Presidential Redwork: A Stitch In Time   Michael G. Buckingham

The son of a successful peanut farmer, James Earl Carter, Jr. was the first American president born in a hospital. He was also the first president from the deep South since before the Civil War. Graduating from the Naval Academy, Carter participated in the development of the nuclear submarine program. He resigned his commission to work the family farm. As governor of Georgia he was known for his civil rights reforms. As president he made the office less formal and emphasized old-fashioned virtues. He was successful in negotiating peace between Israel and Egypt, but the Iran hostage situation crippled his chances for re-election. He is now an active participant in Habitat for Humanity and other humanitarian work.

Notable Quote:
We must adjust to changing times and still hold to unchanging principles.

Jimmy Carter
1977 – 1981

Birthplace: Plains, Georgia
Born: 1924
Party: Democrat
Terms: One
Vice-President: Walter F. Mondale

Moscow Olympics Boycott 1980

1789 — 2001

Jimmy Carter
39th President 1977-1981

Presidential Redwork: A Stitch In Time — Michael G. Buckingham

Ronald Reagan
1981 – 1989

Birthplace: Tampico, Illinois
Born: 1911
Party: Republican
Terms: Two
Vice-President: George Bush

Ronald Reagan's road to the presidency was unlike any other. In high school and college he excelled in three areas – sports, drama, and politics. A short career in sports broadcasting led to a long career as a movie actor. After the war he served six terms as president of the Screen Actors Guild. Previously a Democrat, he switched his affiliation in 1962 to the Republican party. He served two terms as governor of California, and as president, Reagan received more popular votes than any other U.S. President. His second term made him, at 74, the oldest president ever elected. Reagan was wounded in an assassination attempt but quickly recovered. His hawkish attitude and strong foreign policy helped bring an end to the Cold War.

Notable Quote: (in reference to the Berlin Wall)
Mr. Gorbachev, tear down this wall!

First Space Shuttle Launch 1981

1789 — 2001

Ronald Reagan
40th President 1981-1989

George Herbert Walker Bush was the first sitting vice-president to take the presidency by popular vote since Martin Van Buren in 1836. Raised in New England, Bush's father had been a U.S. Senator from Connecticut. Bush was a decorated Navy pilot in World War II, having been shot down and rescued. After the war, he married then moved his family to the oil fields of Texas where he eventually started his own oil company. Successful in business, Bush turned his eye to politics. Among his posts were a seat in the U.S. Congress, U.S. Liaison to China, and Director of the CIA. As president, Bush's popularity ran high during the Persian Gulf War, but he lost his bid for re-election due partly to his unkept promise of "no new taxes."

Notable Quote:
I have spoken of a thousand points of light, of all the community organizations that are spread like stars throughout the Nation...

George Bush
1989 – 1993

Birthplace: Milton, Massachusetts
Born: 1924
Party: Republican
Terms: One
Vice-President: Dan Quayle

Berlin Wall Falls 1989

1789   2001

George Bush
41st President 1989-1993

Presidential Redwork: A Stitch In Time — Michael G. Buckingham — 59

William J. Clinton
1993 – 2001

Birthplace: Hope, Arkansas
Born: 1946
Party: Democrat
Terms: Two
Vice-President: Albert Gore, Jr.

William Jefferson Clinton was America's first "Baby Boomer" president, as well as one of our nation's most controversial presidents. Plagued by accusations of infidelity and wrong-doing throughout his presidency, he became only the second Commander-in-Chief in U.S. history to undergo impeachment proceedings. As with Andrew Johnson before him, there were not enough votes to remove him from office. Clinton grew up in Arkansas and developed an early interest in politics. He won a Rhodes Scholarship to Oxford University and studied law at Yale. At the age of 32 he was the governor of Arkansas, and in 1990 became only the second person in Arkansas political history to be elected to a fifth term.

Notable Quote:
We must do what America does best: offer more opportunity to all and demand responsibility from all.

English Channel Tunnel 1994

1789 — 2001

William J. Clinton
42nd President 1993-2001

Presidential Redwork: A Stitch In Time — Michael G. Buckingham

Historical DESIGNS

Presidential Redwork: A Stitch In Time — Michael G. Buckingham

★ THE GREAT SEAL OF THE UNITED STATES ★

A combination of several designs, the seal was adopted by the Continental Congress on June 20, 1782. Seven years later Congress authorized it as the seal of the United States. The eagle bears a shield without support, signifying that the United States should rely on its own virtues. The olive branch and arrows in the talons refer to the power of peace and war held by Congress. The scroll "E Pluribus Unum" (One Out of Many), the 13 red and white stripes and the constellation of 13 stars all represent a new nation of 13 states.

★ THE 25 CENT EAGLE ★

You can usually find this bird in your purse or pocket. Like the real thing, this eagle is becoming a rare species. Although George Washington's place is secure on the front of the quarter, the noble eagle is gradually being replaced as each state of the Union is being commemorated on newly minted coinage.

★ PRIMITIVE EAGLE ★

This eagle is a "primitive" variation of the eagle of the Great Seal. Besides its simplicity, it is unusual because its wings are directed downward instead of up like most American eagle designs. This is a great pattern for a variety of projects and goes well with a rustic, colonial motif.

★ THE LIBERTY BELL ★

Originally known as the Old State House Bell, it was hung in the tower of the State House in Philadelphia on June 7, 1753. It was rung on July 8, 1776 in Independence Hall to celebrate America's Declaration of Independence. It cracked on July 8, 1835 while tolling for the funeral of Chief Justice John Marshall. It was last rung on Washington's Birthday in 1846, when it cracked even further.

An inscription on the bell reads –
"Proclaim Liberty throughout all the land unto all the inhabitants thereof.– Lev. 25:10"

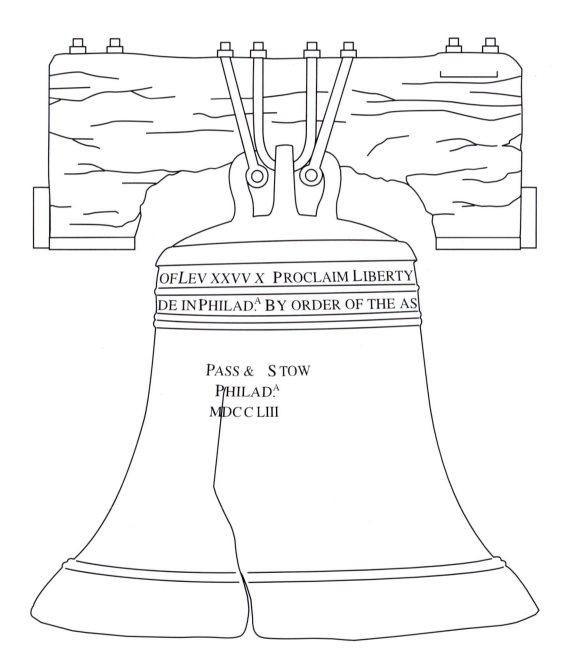

★ GOD BLESS AMERICA ★

America has truly been blessed. Divine Providence has played an important role in the history of the United States. Founded on godly principles, it has been a haven for religious freedom long before it became a nation. Our currency bears the inscription *"In God We Trust."* Our Pledge of Allegiance contains the phrase, *"...one Nation under God...."* Let our hope and desire still be...God bless America!

★ OLD GLORY ★

The first official flag of the United States was established by Congress on June 14, 1777. It consisted of 13 stars and 13 stripes. The original plan was to add stripes as well as stars with the admission of new states. After 15 of each, however, it was evident that this was not going to work. The stripes returned to 13 and it was decided to increase only the number of stars. After the admission of Hawaii in 1959 as the 50th state, the flag was officially changed for the twenty-sixth time since its creation.

*I pledge allegiance to the flag
of the United States of America
and to the Republic for which it stands,
one Nation
under God,
indivisible,
with liberty and justice for all.*

★ THE U.S. CAPITOL BUILDING ★

George Washington laid the cornerstone for the first Capitol structure in 1793. The North Wing was completed in 1800, the South Wing a year later. The buildings were burned by the British in 1814. The center section was finished in 1827, and in two years the original plan was finally completed. In 1851 the cornerstones were laid for the North and South wing extensions and both were occupied by January of 1859. The dome was completed in 1863. The total complex occupies an area of over four acres. Law forbids any structure in the immediate vicinity to rise above it, except for the Washington Monument.

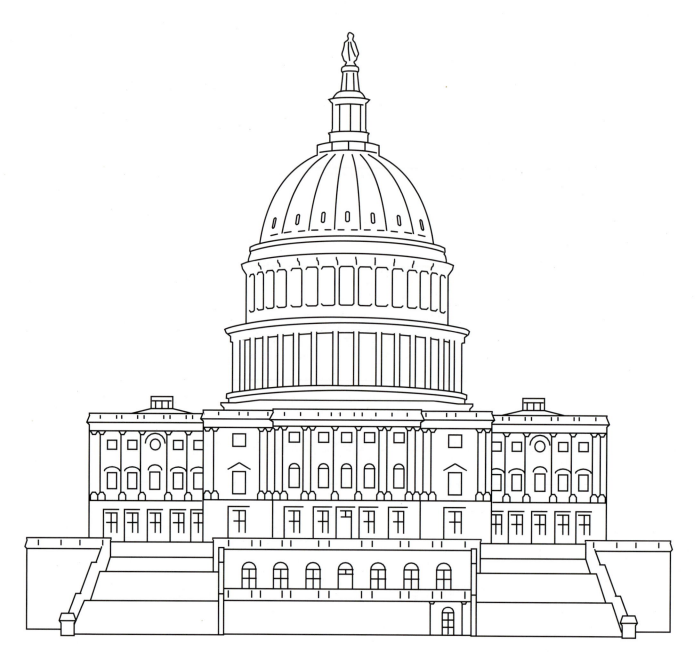

★ THE WHITE HOUSE ★

1600 Pennsylvania Avenue is the official home of the President of the United States. The cornerstone was laid in 1792. Its first resident was second president John Adams. The building was burned by the British on August 24, 1814, and was not reoccupied until December 1817. The White House was renovated in 1902, and except for its outer walls, was completely dismantled and rebuilt in the reconstruction of 1948 – 1952.

★ STARS OF '76 ★

The thirteen stars seen in this configuration were found on a blue field on one of the earliest versions of the American flag. The stars represent the original thirteen colonies that existed when the United States of America declared its independence in 1776. This pattern is excellent for framing inscriptions or making a title block, reduced for a quilt label, or used simply by itself.

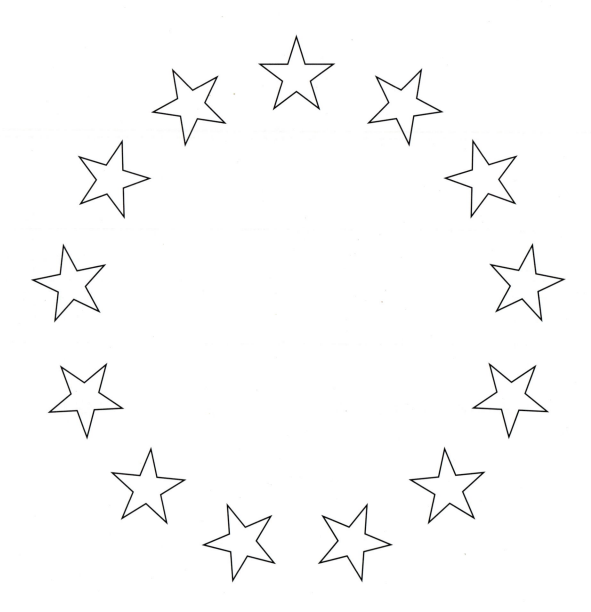

Quilt Settings & PATTERNS

★ Redwork Setting 1 ★

This is a traditional redwork setting, with optional border, and one of the easiest ways to make a quilt top. The blocks are sewn together, with feather stitching applied over the seams (see page 15). This 6 x 7 block setting accommodates all 42 presidential patterns. To include Historical Design patterns, add a seventh row and place these designs in the four corners and in the center three blocks either across the pillow area or middle row of the quilt.

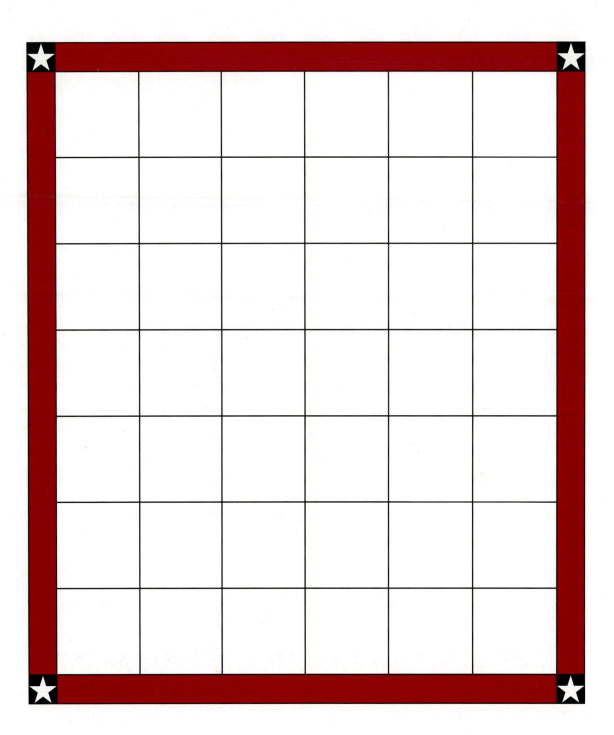

★ Redwork Setting 2 ★

Adding sashing strips is always a popular method for setting blocks together. This setting consists of 9" blocks with 2½" sashing strips and a 3" border. Color recommendations are off-white fabric squares for the blocks, deep red for sashing strips and border, and dark blue corner squares with white stars. The Laurel Leaf machine quilting pattern on page 75 is an excellent way to quilt between and around the blocks. The quilt on page 12 shows a variation of this type of setting.

Presidential Redwork: A Stitch In Time — Michael G. Buckingham

★ Strippy Setting ★

A fresh "new" approach to quiltmaking is the traditional strippy quilt. Framing the blocks with long, wide strips of plain fabric gives you the opportunity to showcase more elaborate quilting. This setting allows space for 42 presidential blocks plus 3 Historical Design blocks in the center row. The quilting patterns can be found on pages 75 – 78.

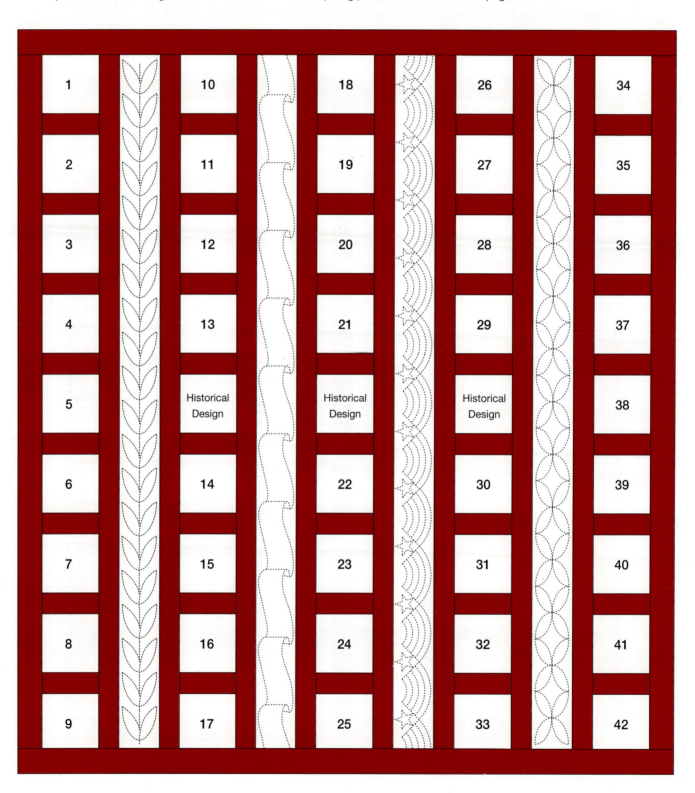

★ Laurel Leaf ★

The laurel garland is associated with victory and leadership, which makes the leaf an appropriate design for a presidential quilt. This machine quilting pattern is easily converted for hand quilting (see page 6).

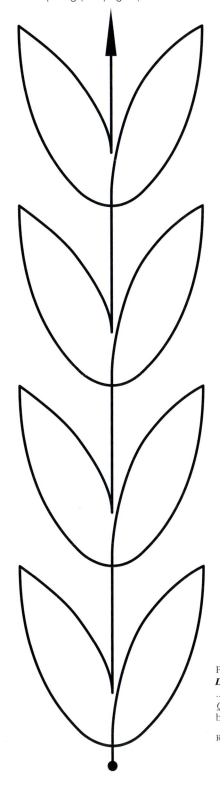

Pattern adapted from ***Daphne's Laurel*** as seen in *...ask Helen – more ABOUT QUILTING DESIGNS*, by Helen Squire (AQS 1990).

Renamed and used with permission.

★ Election Ribbons ★

The ribbon, or banner, is commonly seen flowing from an eagle's beak, with an inscription or motto, but also plays a visual role in political campaigns.

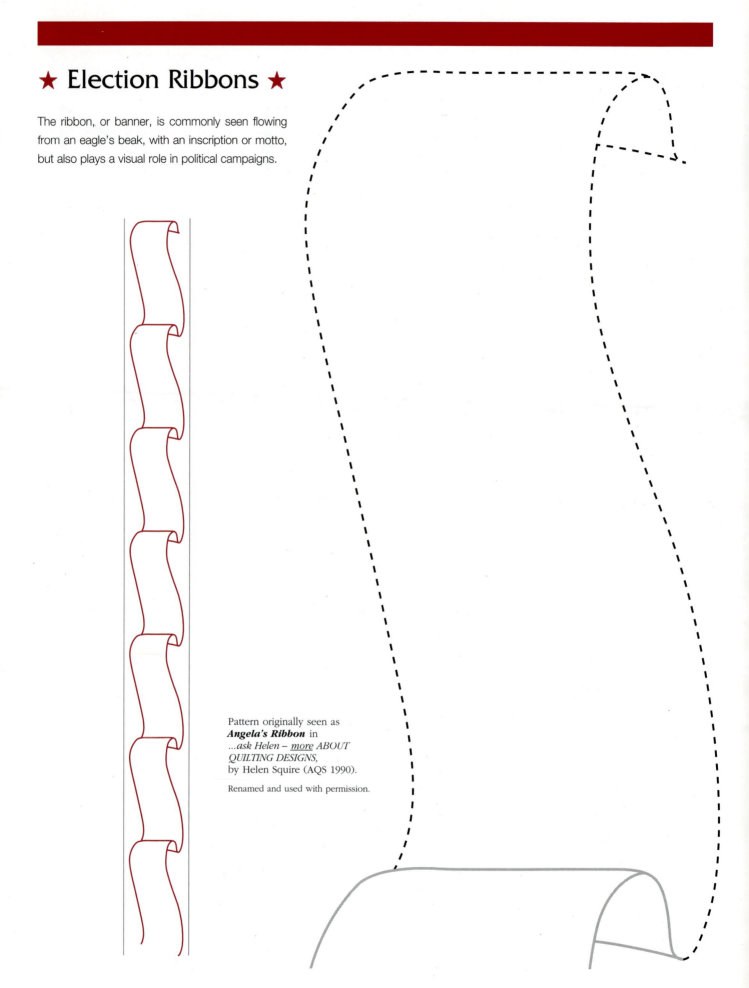

Pattern originally seen as **Angela's Ribbon** in *...ask Helen – more ABOUT QUILTING DESIGNS*, by Helen Squire (AQS 1990).

Renamed and used with permission.

★ Campaign Swag ★

This pattern conjures up images of political rallies and inaugural speeches. The swag is also an important element in traditional appliquéd quilts.

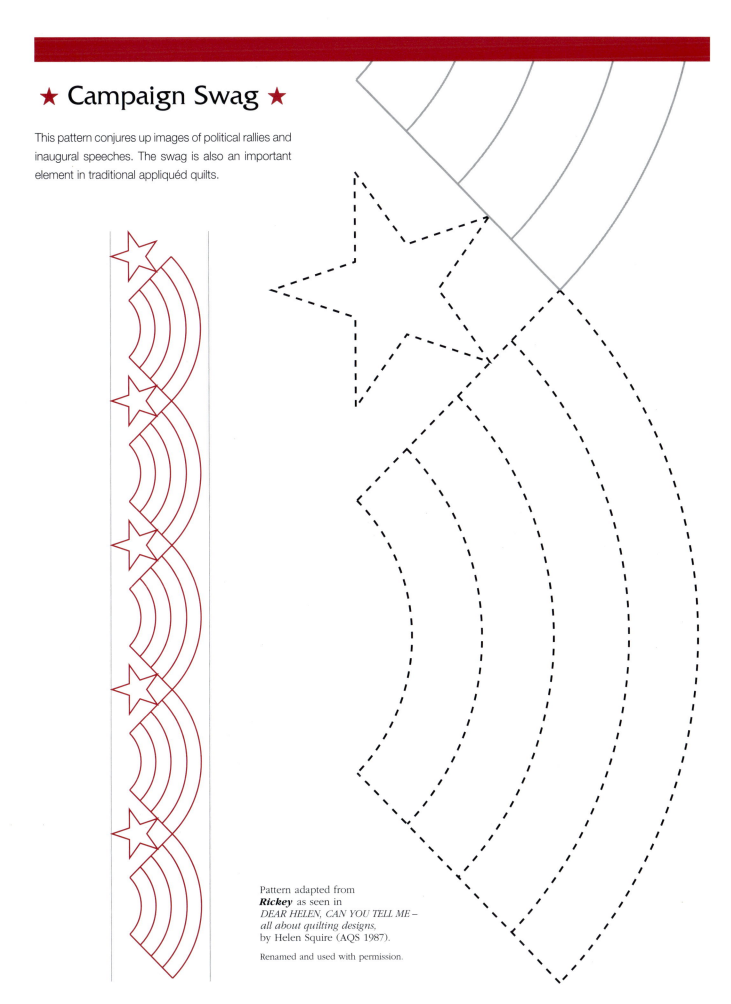

Pattern adapted from ***Rickey*** as seen in *DEAR HELEN, CAN YOU TELL ME – all about quilting designs*, by Helen Squire (AQS 1987).

Renamed and used with permission.

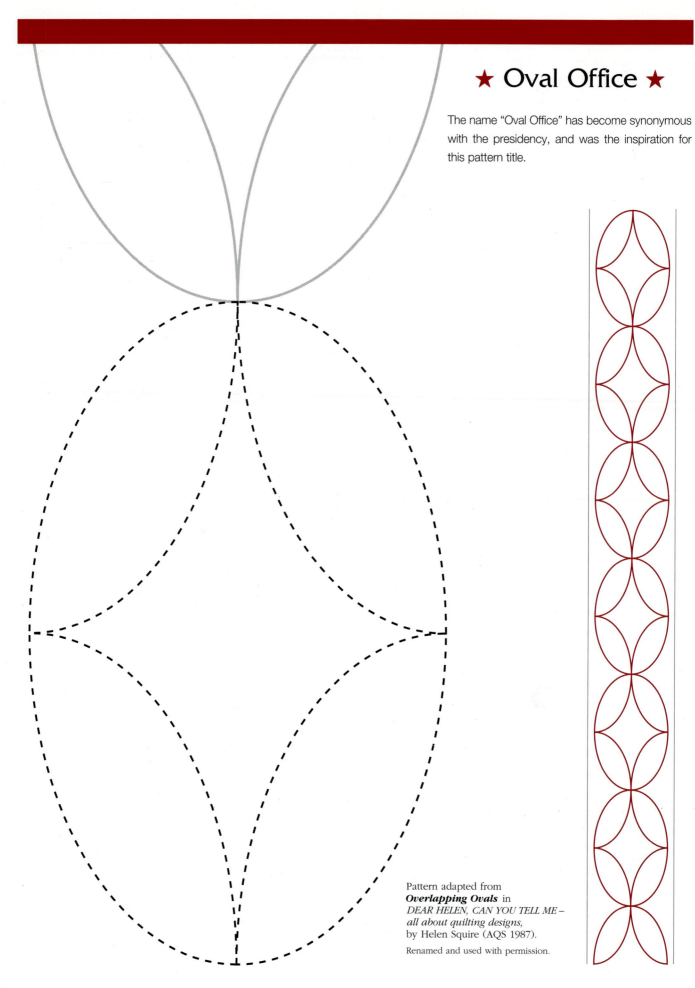

★ Oval Office ★

The name "Oval Office" has become synonymous with the presidency, and was the inspiration for this pattern title.

Pattern adapted from
Overlapping Ovals in
*DEAR HELEN, CAN YOU TELL ME –
all about quilting designs,*
by Helen Squire (AQS 1987).

Renamed and used with permission.

Presidential Redwork: A Stitch In Time Michael G. Buckingham

★★★ BIBLIOGRAPHY ★★★

1. Armbruster, Maxim Ethan. *The Presidents of the United States and Their Administrations from Washington to Nixon*, Horizon Press, 1973.

2. Baranowski, Willa. *Love to Quilt...Historical Penny Squares: Embroidery Patterns*, American Quilter's Society, 1996.

3. Compton's NewMedia, Inc. *Compton's Interactive Encyclopedia*, 1994, 1995.

4. Jones, Cranston. *Homes of the American Presidents*, Bonanza Books, 1962.

5. Lengyel, Cornel Adam. *Presidents of the United States – The Stories of Their Lives*, Golden Press, 1961.

6. Standard Educational Corporation, *New Standard Encyclopedia*, 1982.

The Internet is a great source for presidential information. There are many excellent websites from which to choose. One of the most thorough and comprehensive sites is maintained by the White House at:

www.whitehouse.gov/WH/glimpse/presidents/html/presidents.html

ABOUT THE AUTHOR –

Michael Buckingham has lived and traveled around the U.S. and Europe working as a graphic designer, illustrator, and cartoonist. Combining his interests in design, history, and quilting, he has created this unique book that quilters and their families can both enjoy. An avid sailor, Michael now resides in western Kentucky's lakes area with his wife and two sons.